Alfred Sandham

Montreal and its Fortifications

Alfred Sandham

Montreal and its Fortifications

ISBN/EAN: 9783337327484

Printed in Europe, USA, Canada, Australia, Japan

Cover: Foto ©Andreas Hilbeck / pixelio.de

More available books at **www.hansebooks.com**

MONTREAL,

AND   ITS

FORTIFICATIONS;

BY

ALFRED SANDHAM,

AUTHOR OF COINS OF CANADA, MONTREAL PAST AND PRESENT, &c., &c.

FOR PRIVATE CIRCULATION ONLY.

MONTREAL:

DANIEL ROSE, 210 ST. JAMES STREET.
PRINTER TO THE NUMISMATIC AND ANTIQUARIAN SOCIETY.
1874.

To

J. M. LEMOINE, ESQ.,

OF QUEBEC,

AUTHOR OF "MAPLE LEAVES," ETC.,

THIS WORK

IS RESPECTFULLY DEDICATED

BY

Alf Sandham

LIST OF ILLUSTRATIONS.

FULL PAGE.

WOOD CUTS.

Plate 1.

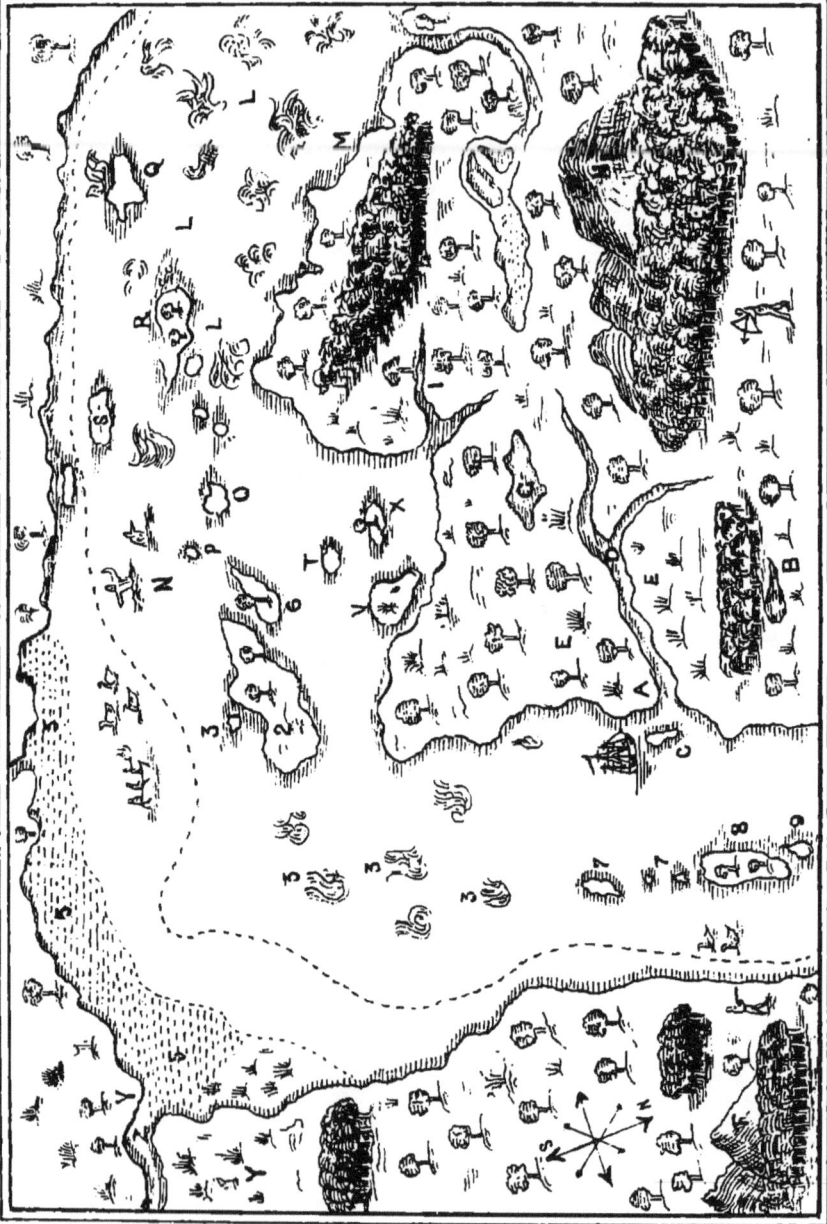

CHAMPLAIN'S MAP OF PART OF THE ISLAND OF MONTREAL.

MONTREAL;

FORTIFICATIONS.

————— •◦•◦• —————

S an Art, fortification is very nearly as ancient as the existence of Society. " When men first assembled together for the purpose of mutual pro. tection, and placed their habitations on the same spot, the law of necessity, springing in this case out of the principle of self defence, rendered it indispensible for them to adopt some means for securing their families, and their property against the sudden inroads of enemies. In early ages, men considered themselves as sufficiently protected by a single wall, from behind which they could with safety discharge their darts, arrows, and other missiles against an assailant ; but when, in the progress of improvement, new and more powerful means of attack were discovered, it became necessary to increase, in a corresponding degree the means of resistance, and accordingly the feeble defensive structures of the primitive ages were in time succeeded by solid ramparts, flanked and commanded by elevated towers."*

* Encyclopædia Britannica.

The savages of America, like those of other lands usually adopted as a means of defence, a circular palisade, a form which appears to have been adhered to by many of the tribes which inhabited that portion of America, now comprised within the limits of the Dominion of Canada. When Jacques Cartier* in 1535, first visited the island whereon now stands the City of Montreal, he found it inhabited by a tribe of Indians, who had established themselves near the foot of the Mountain, which he named Mount Royal.† Here they had erected their cabins or lodges, about 50 in number, the whole being encircled with a palisade formed of the trunks of trees set in a triple row. The outer and inner ranges inclined till they met and crossed near the summit,

SECTION OF INDIAN PALISADE.

while the upright row between them, aided by transverse braces, gave to the whole an abundant strength. Within were galleries for the defenders, rude ladders to mount them, and magazines of stones to throw down on the heads of the assailants. ‡ The entrance was a narrow portal, barely sufficient to admit the bodies of the savages who dwelt with-

* Jacques Cartier, the discoverer of Canada, was born at St. Malo, in France, in 1500. On the 15th May, 1634, he sailed from his native city, on his first voyage to America, returning to France in August of the same year. He made a second voyage in 1535, and on the festival of St. Lawrence, he reached the entrance of the river, which he named in honor of the Saint. In September, he reached Stadacona (Quebec), and in October visited Hochelaga (Montreal), and shortly after returned to France. In 1541, as second in command to DeRoberval, he again visited Canada, and died shortly after his return to France. See Autograph, Plate 2, fig. 1.

† See Frontispiece.

‡ Pioneers of France in the New World.—*Parkman.*

PLATE 2.

FIG. 1.

Cartier

FIG. 2.

Champlain —

FIG. 3.

Paul de Chomedey.

De maisonneufue

FIG. 4.

Riballieus

FIG. 5.

Jeanne Mance

in these, the first fortifications on the Island of Montreal. The palisades must have enclosed a large area, as Cartier states that each of the 50 oblong dwellings were fifty yards or more in length, and 12 or 15 wide, while in the centre of the town was an open area, or public square, a stone's-throw in width. The population was also numerous, as in each of the dwellings resided many families.

How long those primitive fortifications withstood the attacks made by hostile tribes, we know not, and Champlain*who visited the island in 1609 and 1611 makes no mention of them. It was during Champlain's second visit that he chose a site on the island, and cleared ground for a proposed trading post.†The spot chosen was immediately above a small stream (now covered by Commissioner Street and St. Anns Market) which entered the St. Lawrence at what is now known as Pointe à Callière.‡ Here, on the margin of the stream, in order to test the effects of the ice shove, he erected the first wall built on the island with mortar and bricks, the bricks being made from clay found near the spot.§ On, or near this spot, 31 years later, landed the intrepid Maisonneuve,‖ and his little band of ardent followers—" The grain of mustard

* Samuel de Champlain was a native of Brouage in France. In 1603-07, he explored the St. Lawrence from Tadousac to Three Rivers. On the 3rd July, 1608, he laid the foundation of Quebec. Under successive Vice-Roys he continued to act as Lieutenant, and in 1627 the Vice Royalty was suspended, and Champlain was appointed first Governor of New France. He died on Christmas day, 1635, deeply regretted by the Colonists. See Autograph, Plate 2, fig.2.

† See plate 1.

‡ So called after the Chevalier Hector de Calliere, a native of Torigny in Normandy, who came to Canada as a member of the Montreal Trading Company, and was appointed Governor of the City. In 1698 he succeeded Frontenac as Governor of New France, and held the appointment until 1703. The great wisdom manifested by him during his term of office endeared him to the people. In 1701 he concluded a favorable treaty (at Montreal) with the Indians, thereby securing a long term of peace. See Autograph, Plate 2, figure 4.

§ Very fine clay for brick making was formerly taken in large quantities from the neighbourhood of this site and through Griffintown.

‖ Paul Chomedey Sieur De Maisonneuve, founder of Montreal, of whose early history but little has been handed down to the present, was its first Governor. In 1647, he was, at his own request, replaced by M. d'Ailleboust. For his valuable services to the Church of Rome in Canada, a pension was conferred upon him by the Seminary at Paris. See Autograph, Plate 2, figure 3.

seed that was to grow until its branches overshadowed the land." May 18th, 1642, was the birth day of Ville Marie, as Montreal was named by its pious founders. It was a wild, yet beautiful scene which lay before their view, but they knew full well that amid the green woods which surrounded them, there were foes against whom they must defend themselves, and their first thought was to erect their homes with a view to mutual protection. Their dwellings were built closely together, and the whole was surrounded by palisades of wood and stone, known as the Fort and Château of Ville Marie,* and it was immediately outside these walls that the first Hospital (under the management of Mademoiselle Mance†) was erected, and likewise enclosed with palisades.

The Fort was the scene of many attacks by the Indians, and at times it was dangerous to pass beyond the palisades. In front of its walls, Maisonneuve proved to his followers that while he desired their safety, he himself was no coward, but ready if needs be, to face single handed the savage hordes. Near this fort was also erected a windmill for the use of the colonists. The fort gradually fell into decay ‡ and the remaining portion of timber and stone was used in the erection of part of the first Parish Church in Place d'Armes

* The fort was built of wood, and was constructed by Maisonneuve, in accordance with plans made under the direction of M. Louis D'Ailleboust, Governor of Canada.—*Viger's Notes to Dollier de Casson's His. of Montreal, published by the Montreal His. Soc. pp. 228.* M. Louis D'Ailleboust was appointed Governor of Canada in 1647. He was of German descent. He came to Canada, but a short time anterior to his appointment, with about 100 Colonists ; bringing also with him his wife and sister. Replaced by De Lauzon in 1651, he settled in the Country, and died at Quebec in 1660. See Autograph, Plate 4, fig. 1. For plan of the Fort and Chateau, see Plate 3.

† Mademoiselle Mance was a descendant of an ancient family in France. She accompanied Maisonneuve and his party to Montreal, for the purpose of superintending the hospital which the Colonists had decided to erect on their arrival. At this time she was 34 years of age, and although of delicate constitution, was ready to face any hardship, so that she might spread the cause of her Church. See Autograph, Plate 2, fig. 5.

‡ On or near this site DeCalliere subsequently erected his private residence, known as the Chateau Calliere. Mr. Viger in his Notes to the History of Montreal, says, that in his early days he had seen traces of the old fortifications at Point a Calliere.

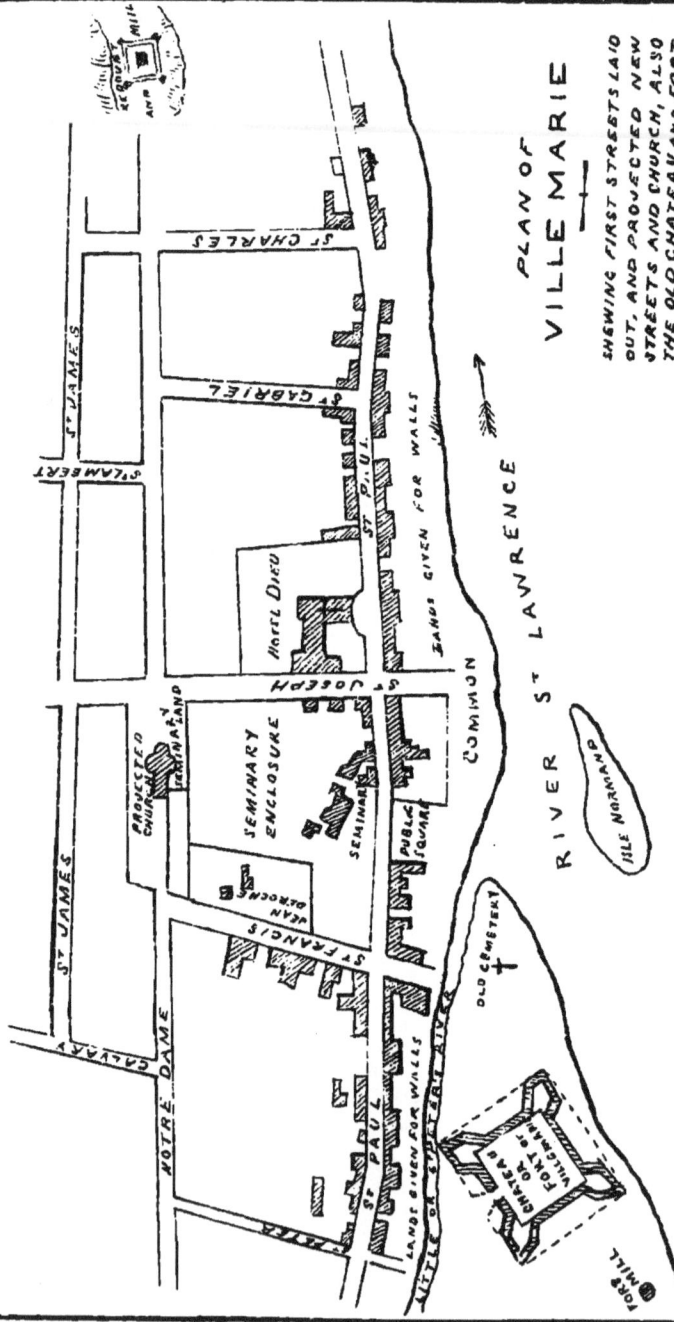

PLATE 5.

PLAN OF
VILLE MARIE

SHEWING FIRST STREETS LAID
OUT, AND PROJECTED NEW
STREETS AND CHURCH, ALSO
THE OLD CHATEAU AND FORT.

RIVER ST LAWRENCE

ISLE NORMAND

COMMON

LANDS GIVEN FOR WALLS

ST PAUL

ST CHARLES

ST GABRIEL

HOTEL DIEU

ST JOSEPH

SEMINARY ENCLOSURE

SEMINARY

PUBLIC SQUARE

PROJECTED CHURCH

SEMINARY LAND

JEAN DESROCHES

ST FRANCIS

ST JAMES

ST LAMBERT

ST JAMES

CALVARY

NOTRE DAME

ST PAUL

LANDS GIVEN FOR WALLS

LITTLE ST LAURENT RIVER

OLD CEMETERY

CHATEAU DE LONGUE VILLE

FORT HILL

RECOLLET MILL AND FORT

in 1672.* As years rolled by, the demands of the increasing

OLD ROMAN CATHOLIC PARISH CHURCH, PLACE D'ARMES.

population required the erection of another Mill at the eastern extremity of the town, as laid out by Maisonneuve. Accordingly an elevation at the lower end of Notre Dame Street† was chosen and about the year 1680, the mill was erected, and surrounded by a wall, which continued to serve as a a battery for the defence of the town, the " guns commanding the whole extent of the streets from one end to the other."‡ Of the final demolition of this fort I shall speak hereafter, and shall now proceed to review the events which

---

* "For the erection of this Church, contributions of money, material or labor were proffered, and the priests of the Seminary resolved to demolish the Chateau and fort of Ville Marie, which was falling into ruins, and to use the timber and stone in the new building."

† Now Dalhousie Square.   ‡ See Plate 5.

led to the erection of fortifications of sufficient extent to enclose the town itself,   In 1664, the English acquired possession of the Province of New York, and being desirous of making
as much as possible out of their new acquisition, they sought,
and obtained, a large portion of the fur trade which had hither-
to been wholly centred in Montreal.   The success which attended their efforts led to much jealousy between them and
the French.   To secure themselves in the matter, the English
managed to retain as allies and friends, the powerful Iro-
quois, who proved of great service in repelling the incursions
of the French.   As the French settlements increased, the
colonists assumed offensive operations on the New England
frontier, and the spirit of the British being roused, the result
was that both parties, aided by the Indians, carried on a de-
structive warfare.   Montreal naturally became the point of
attack, and to protect the town, the Governor, M. de Callière
determined to erect fortifications. He issued orders, in 1684,
to the inhabitants, requiring them to cut down, and bring in
large stakes of cedar.   To this order a ready response was
given, the inhabitants having worked so vigorously during the winter of that year, that early in the spring of
1685 six hundred men were started to work in erect-
ing the palisade.   This when completed, rose about
15 feet above the ground, with watch towers, platforms, and
a gate, so that the place might be shut and guarded.   For
this work the inhabitants were compelled to furnish the stakes,
which were then put up at the expense of the King.*   As
might be expected, these wooden erections did not prove
very durable, and repairs had to be made each year.

In 1713, by the treaty of Utrecht, peace was ensured to
France, and as a natural result, the resources of the colony in
New France were greatly developed.   It was now (1713) resolved to construct in the future, the enclosure at Montreal, in
stone, and in lieu of furnishing the stakes for the wooden pali-

* The red line in Plate 6 shews the line of these Palisades.

PLATE 4

Fig 1.

D'Ailleboust

Fig. 2

De Ramezay

Fig 3

L A de Bourbon

Fig 4

Le marechal d'estrées

Fig 5

Par Le Conseil

Lachapelle

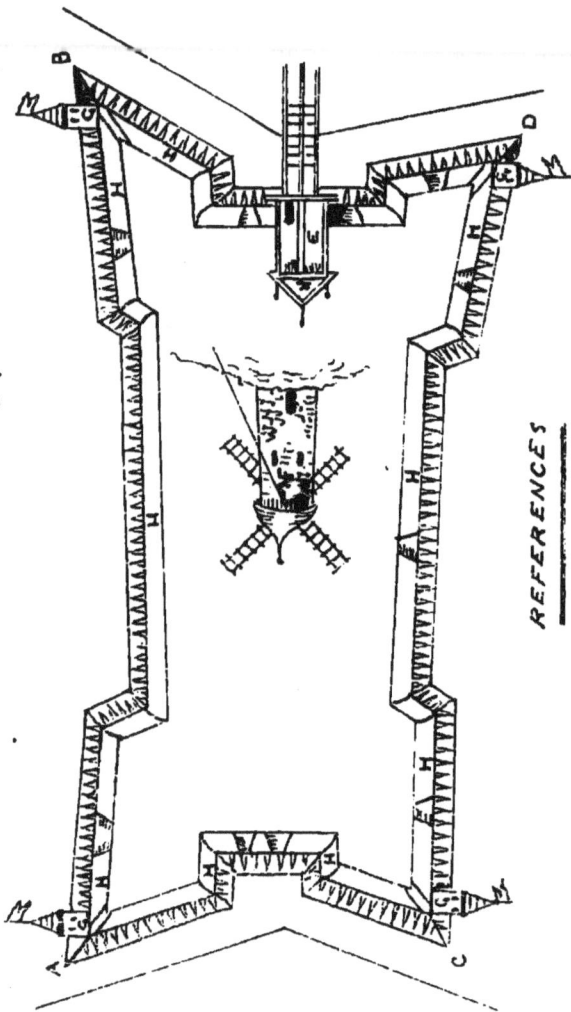

PLATE 6.

FORT AND WINDMILL ON CITADEL HILL, (NOW DALHOUSIE SQUARE.)

REFERENCES

EXTENT OF WALLS FROM A TO B,-218 FT; A TO C- 88; C TO D-202 FT; B TO D-108 FT.

E-ENTRANCE: F-MILL; G.G.G.G. SMALL TOWERS; H- WALLS.

sade, it was ordered that a portion of the expense of the new
walls should be paid by the inhabitants. The Engineer upon
whom devolved the duty of preparing plans for the new works,
was M. Chaussegros de Lery, who submitted two plans, one of
which followed to some extent the lines of the wooden palisades, cutting off a portion of the town as then laid out. The
plan adopted was that shewn in plate 6, which was recom-
mended by him on the ground " that it will not be more ex-
pensive than the other, while it will be incomparably better for defensible purposes." To provide for the erection of
the new fortifications, an act was passed in May, 1716, author-
izing M. de Ramezay, Governor of Montreal,* to proceed with
the work, and for the purpose about 300,000 livres were to be
advanced by the French King. One half of this sum was to
be charged to His Majesty's account, while the other half was
to be paid by the Seminary, (Siegneurs of the Island.) and
the Inhabitants. The Seminary to pay yearly 2000 livres, and
the citizens 4000 until the amount was paid off. Officers of
the Army, and any others in the King's service were exempt
from the tax. This tax was cheerfully paid by the inhabitants,
but the Seminary objected to the proportion charged them†
but without avail. They urged in their petition that " the
tax had been made with little equity, since it levied 2000 livres
yearly, which is the third of the whole tax, instead of which
the Seminary ought not to pay the hundredth part of it in proportion to the number of those who are liable to pay." They
also urged that they should be relieved on the grounds that
they had " engaged to make large expenditure for the trans-
portation and establishment of a mission among the Indians
along the Lake of the Two Mountains." The French Counsel,
however, viewed the matter in a different light, and in reply

* Claude de Ramezay, Seigneur of la Gesse, Knight of the Military Order of St. Louis, was
appointed Governor of Montreal in 1703. His son, J. Bpt. Nicholas Roch de Ramezay, signed
the Capitulation of Quebec. See Autograph, Plate 4, fig. 2.

† Canadian MSS., pp. 667, 23rd May, 1720.

spoke of the manner in which the assessment had been made, and further stated :

"It is in view of that decree that the tax has been made, the Seminary however pretend to ignore it, although it had full knowledge of it before and after, and the counsel remember the trouble that theAbbé de St.Aubin took formerly to hinder it." The counsel does not think that anything which has been done ought to be changed.

(Signed,)   L. A. DE BOURBON.

LE MARECHAL D'ESTREES.*

In 1717, (18th August), De Lery forwarded to France a lengthy report as to the advantages offered by Montreal for the purpose of fortifications. From it we gather the following interesting facts as to the condition of the town at the time named, and also of the proposed improvements. Reference to plate 6, will explain some of the principal points referred to by him. "The town of Montreal is very extensive, its circumference is three quarters of a league, its fortification having 1819 toises (fathoms) enclosed. It is enclosed only by a poor enclosure of stakes, a part of which are rotten. The inhabitants, have made in it several openings, and there is no door in a state to be shut. It is not shut during the whole year, and as we are in this country exposed every day to be at war with the English, and with the Indians, and as we cannot hear of the declaration of war in Europe, except after the English, they could very easily take the town in the state in which it is. What remains of the enclosure of stakes will last at most four or five years. Therefore I have determined to commence an enclosure capable to resist the artillery that the English might bring from Orange.† If I had commenced it weaker, it would be no good for defence, and no advantage. The ground gets frozen so deep in this country that a wall alone can last any time.

---

* See Autographs, Plate 4, figs. 3-4.   † Now Albany.

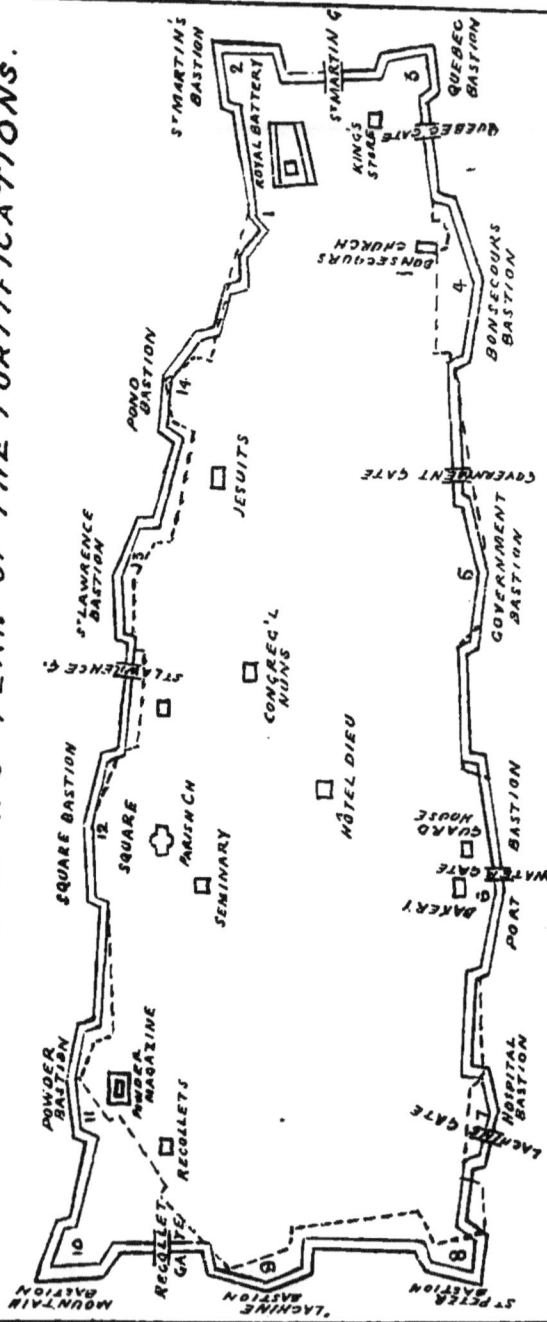

CHAUSSEGROS DE LERY'S PLAN OF THE FORTIFICATIONS.

PLATE 6.

THE FIGURES REFER TO SECTIONS OF STONE WALLS. SEE PLATE 7.
THE RED DOTTED LINE ---- MARKS OUTLINE OF DeCALLIERE'S WOODEN PALLISADES.

St MARTIN'S BASTION
ROYAL BATTERY
St MARTIN'S G.
KING'S STORE
QUEBEC GATE
QUEBEC BASTION
BONSECOURS CHURCH
BONSECOURS BASTION
POND BASTION
JESUITS
GOVERNMENT GATE
GOVERNMENT BASTION
St LAWRENCE BASTION
St LAWRENCE G.
CONGREG'L NUNS
HÔTEL DIEU
SQUARE BASTION
SQUARE
PARISH CH
SEMINARY
GUARD HOUSE
WATER GATE
BAKERY
PORT BASTION
POWDER BASTION
POWDER MAGAZINE
RECOLLET'S
RECOLLET'S GATE
HOSPITAL BASTION
LACHINE GATE
MOUNTAIN BASTION
LACHINE BASTION
St PETER BASTION

"I have been obliged to commence a ditch. The Governors did not wish that any should be made, and that the enclosure should be made weaker than the one began. The council will see by the sections annexed to the plans* that the walls of the revetment are reduced only to three feet in thickness, which is the smallest thickness which can be given to the least fortification.

"The nature of the ground requires that the foundations should be very deep; but a great deal of the stone dug out of the foundation serves to build the revetment. The earth from the ditch is used to make a rampart, and thereby the thickness of the wall may be made less, and the fortification is better, being made according to the rules.

"According to calculation, the enclosure made with a ditch, will cost half what it would, had it been made high up on the ground without a ditch. I have commenced on the Lachine gate, it being the side of attack.

"There are some houses on the edge of a little stream†which is dry during the summer, and which can be crossed during the winter on the ice. The Governors would like that these houses should serve in the enclosure of the town; but it is not according to the rules that private houses should serve to enclose a city. Those houses having doors and windows which would open outside of the town, the proprietors might be at liberty to introduce the enemy into the place, and cause to enter or let out whom they should like. Moreover, those houses would break the road around the walls, which would hinder the watch to the security of the place, and again, that place would be without defense, which has always been against the orders of the King, and against the regulations he has made, his intention being that the road around be free, that a place should be defended everywhere, and that a large space should be left between the enclosure of a town, and the houses. I cause the enclosure to pass before those houses, as the ground permits it, but as the Governors wish that those houses should serve in the enclosure, I beg very humbly the council to decide.

" I have seen a regulation of M. the Marshal de Vauban's, in which it was ordered that Engineers shall inform the court about the difficulties met in working fortifications, the court reserving to itself the decision about the matter.

" The situation of this town is advantageous and easy to fortify. I do not see that the surrounding country can inconvenience its fortifications. It is large, and there are many buildings going up, and the inhabitants commence to want sites to build houses, which fact shews it has been badly laid out, and even too much enlarged. It is now full of gardens which are useless in the midst of a town, and render the enclosure of the streets too large. Twice as many streets might easily be made, and thereby give sites to build houses.

I have marked the plan of those streets, one of which will be more than a quarter of a league in length.* It appears to me necessary to settle those streets in order that they might be built upon, and that those who build should do it in such a way that it might not be necessary afterwards to make them move to cut other streets. I have the honor to send the plan to the council, and I shall wait for its decision.

It will be necessary to remove some houses which are marked on the plan, and it seems just that the owners of them should be indemnified. The Council might grant them some permits for commerce to Detroit or Michilimackinac.

" I have marked a Place d'Armes† in front of the *(paroisse)* Parish Church, where might be made afterwards a number of barracks, the houses which are in that place being of small value.

The enclosure is marked upon the ground conformably to

---

* St. Paul Street.   † See Plate 6.

PLATE 7.

BASTIONS
9. TO 13.

BASTIONS 2 AND 14.

BASTIONS ON
RIVER FRONT.
3 TO 8

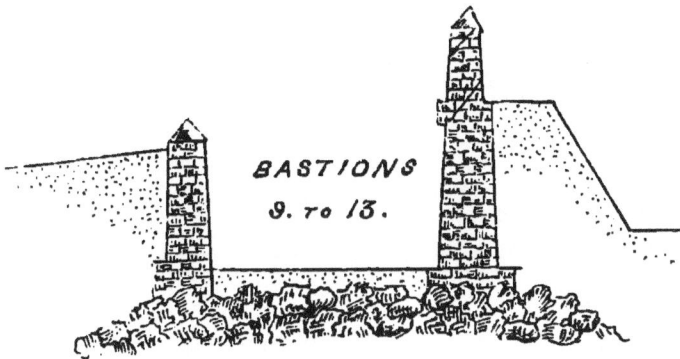

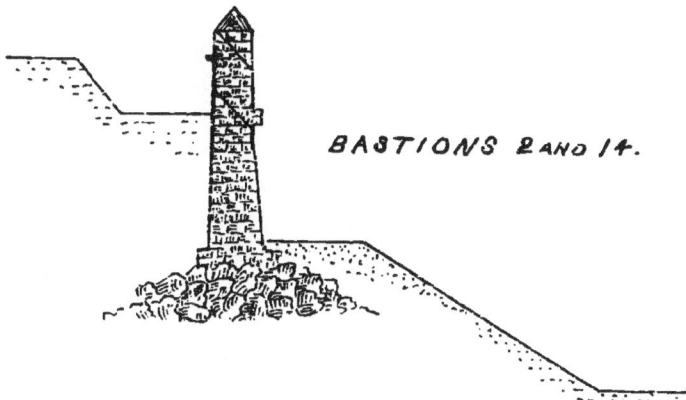

ELEVATIONS OF FORTIFICATIONS ERECTED
BY CHAS. DE LERY.

the plan.   I have stockaded all the angles in a permanent
way, at a certain height, on the side of the River.

" The powder magazine* of this town is bad.   The wall is
open in some places, and it is covered with a wooden roof.

" I have marked on the plan a powder magazine on the
top of the hill.†

Done at Montreal, the 10th of August, 1717.

(Signed,)   CHAUSSEGROS DE LERY.

During the same year, De Lery commenced the work, but
from lack of funds it was discontinued, and for some years
nothing of consequence was done.   In 1718, a sum
of 15,000 livres was voted for the erection of Prisons and
Court Houses in Montreal and Quebec, and De Lery vainly
endeavored to induce the Government to assign a portion of
the amount towards the continuance of his work, urging that
if these funds were in hard cash, it was more than enough
to build the prisons, and he " begs the Council that the
amount it will be able to get from that fund, after the prisons are made, be employed in the fortifications of the enclosure of Montreal.   " If the Council were to grant that
amount of 15000 livres, for the said enclosure, to commence
in 1719, and the said amount added to 4,000 livres which the
inhabitants of the town give, and 4,000 from the priests of
the Seminary of St. Sulpice, who are the Seigneurs of the
whole island, and whose income would be more than sufficient for the keeping of the priests.   These gentlemen do
not give much, only 2,000 livres for the enclosure, and the
Council gives them, I am told, 6,000 livres yearly.   That sum
might be employed toward the fortification of the city ; and
as at Quebec a garrison for the guard of the castle is useless,
since there is none, the funds appropriated for that purpose
would certainly be better employed for the security of the
colony in the construction of the enclosure of the City of
Montreal, than for the private benefit of the person who gets

---

* See Plate 6.   † Citadel Hill, now Dalhousie Square. See "Royal Battery," Plate 6

it. The funds taken from the Seminary of Montreal, and those from the garrison of the Castle of Quebec, as well as the contribution levied upon the inhabitants, (and it is imposed with equity : each inhabitant having to pay in proportion to his income. It is certain that this sum, if it was contributed by every inhabitant equally, would not amount to more than five or six livres each), will make a total, namely :

From the Council 15,000
    "   Seminary of St. Sulpice 6,000
    "   Garrison of the Castle of Quebec 7,000
    "   The Inhabitants of Montreal 8,000
    "   Some leases 4,000

                    Total............... 40,000

which would be sufficient to enclose the City of Montreal with an enclosure as it has been approved of by the Council, in five years."

The Council did not entertain De Lery's proposal, and the original document now lies in Paris, with a marginal note thereon, as follows : " *En delibere*,—intended to shew him the impossibility of what he proposes.

                              LA CHAPELLE."*

During the years which elapsed, up to 1721, no progress was made, as we learn from DeLery's report for that year, wherein he says : " I have not had the work continued since 1717, for want of money. I have merely taken about twenty stakes from a salient angle where the wall passes, which the contractor has used for scaffolding, according to contract of the 8th of May, 1717, the original of which is in France, in the bureau of the Colonies, Those stakes are to be sold in behalf of the new enclosure when near ready.

" I have the honor to represent to the Council that the Governors have taken a very great interest in the preser-

---

* See Autograph, Plate 4, No. 5.

PLATE 8

FIG. 1.

Beyon

FIG. 2.

Amherst

FIG. 3.

Vaudreuil

FIG. 4.

Rich.ᵈ Montgomery

FIG.

J. N. Rhondelet

FIG. 6.

John Richardson

FIG. 7.

Dalhousie

FIG. 8. *Votre plus obligée et obeissante*
Servante Marguerite Bourgeoys

vation of the fortifications ; and, it has happened, that when regiments, and the inhabitants of the towns, have caused damage to the fortifications, the troops have been admonished, and the inhabitants have repaired what they had damaged.

" I beg the Council to give orders that whatever may be damaged or carried away, be replaced at the expense of those who do it, and to order me to apprise the Council of it, which is the only means to prevent, in this Colony, the ruin of the fortifications, otherwise it will cost a great deal to His Majesty every year, as has already happened, to replace what has been taken away, and to make good the damage. The same order must be understood in regard to the King's buildings, artillery, &c.

" It is also necessary, that the Town of Montreal be shut up and guarded, as it was formerly, until it is fortified with walls."

In 1721, the work was fairly entered upon, and De Lery spent the greater part of the summer at Montreal, superintending the work.

As the work progressed, considerable difficulty was experienced in negotiating with the inhabitants for the land on which the walls were to be erected.* Accordingly in 1726, M. Begon† the Intendant, issued an order requiring all proprietors of the lands to bring their titles of property to M. Rambault, (*Procureur du Roi,*) that an estimate of their value might be made. The owners, however, had but little confidence in the official honesty of the day, and no attention was paid to the order, and in 1726, Begon, in his despatch, expresses his belief that the inhabitants " perhaps feared that they will be re-imbursed only according to the amount of their deeds, the lands having greatly increased in value since they have had possession of them." The Intendant, however, was not to be hindered in this manner, and

---

* Vaudreuil's Despatches.   † See Autograph, Plate 8. fig. 1.

therefore, notwithstanding the want of the title deeds, he appointed Commissioners* to set a value upon them, according to the knowledge they had of the same. Of course this plan caused dissatisfaction, which, however, was of little avail, for the land was *expropriated*, and the work upon the walls steadily progressed until they were finally completed.

The fortifications were somewhat formidable in appearance, although subsequent events proved them to be of but little real value, nor were they destined to pass through any ordeal calculated to test their durability.

In 1747, a celebrated traveller,† who visited the town, describes it as being "well fortified, surrounded by a high and thick wall. In front runs the River, while on the other sides is a deep ditch, filled with water, which secures the inhabitants against all danger from sudden incursions of the enemy. It cannot, however, stand a long siege, as on account of its extent, it would require a large garrison. The gates are numerous, there being five on the river side."

Fortunately the inhabitants were not exposed to much danger or suffering at the hands of an enemy, and we question whether any fortified city ever fell more easily into the hands of its captors, than did the good City of Montreal, when on the morning of the 18th of September 1760, Amherst's‡ army entered with colors flying and drums beating, to take possession of its forts and towers, and on that day from its walls was thrown to the breeze the red banner of England.

In view of the following letter from a French officer, can

---

* M. Rambault and M. Degue.   † Professor Kalm of the University of Abo in Sweden.
‡ Jeffrey, Lord Amherst, was born in Kent, England, January 29th, 1717. He entered the Army in 1731. In 1758, (16th March), he sailed from Portsmouth, as Major-General, having command of the troops destined for the seige of Louisbourg, which place he captured on the 26th of July following. In 1759 he commanded one of the armies formed for the conquest of Canada. Having captured several minor forts, Montreal surrendered to his army, on the 8th September, 1760. He continued in command in Canada until 1763, when he returned to England. For his gallant services he was (in 1776) created Baron Amherst of Holmdale in Kent, and in 1782 received another Patent as Baron Amherst of Montreal. He died (leaving no issue) at his seat in Kent, August 3, 1791. See Autograph, Plate 8, fig. 2.

PLATE 9.

PLAN OF MONTREAL IN 1759.

we wonder that the brave Vaudreuil * should have accepted the terms proposed.† No more desperate position
could be conceived. The writer states : " We were shut up in
Montreal. Amherst's army appeared in sight on the side
towards the Lachine gate, on the 7th September, about 3
in the afternoon, and General Murray, with his army from
Quebec appeared two hours after at the opposite side of the
town. Thus the black crisis was at hand for the fate of
Canada. Montreal was no ways susceptible of a defence.
It was surrounded with walls, built with design only to pre-
serve the inhabitants from the incursions of the Indians, little imagining at that time, that it would become the theatre
of a regular war, and that one day they would see formidable armies of regular well disciplined troops before its walls.
We were, however, all pent up in that miserable bad place,
without provisions, a thousand times worse than a position
in an open field, whose pitiful walls could not resist two hours
cannonade, without being levelled to the ground, and when
we would have been forced to surrender at discretion if the
English had insisted upon it. The night between the 7th
and 8th was passed in negotiating for the Articles of Capitulation. But in the morning all the difficulties were removed, and Gen. Amherst accorded conditions infinitely
more favorable than could be expected in the circumstances."‡

Whatever value the French inhabitants may have placed
upon their stone walls, the troops do not appear to have
placed much faith in them as a means of defence, and after
the capitulation to the English, the new rulers paying but little

---

* Marquis de Vaudreuil, the last Governor of Canada under French Regime, was born at
Quebec in 1698. While comparatively young, he entered the military service, and speedily
rose to the rank of Major. In 1733, he was appointed Governor of Three Rivers, and in 1743
of Louisiana : being exceedingly popular in both positions. In 1748 he succeeded to his
father's title, and in 1755 was appointed Governor of Canada, in which position he continued
until the capitulation of Montreal in 1760. He died in France in 1764. See Autograph, Plate
8, fig. 3.

† See Appendix A.

‡ See Plan of Montreal at time of conquest, Plate 9, and View of Montreal in 1760, from
a rare print, Plate 10.

attention to them, they gradually fell into decay, and.

RARE MEDAL, BEARING A VIEW OF MONTREAL IN 1760.*

when in 1775, Montgomery† and the American troops appeared in front of the town, and demanded its surrender,
the citizens, although knowing full well that their ruined
walls would prove no defence, determined to enforce, if possible, the observance of military custom ere they surrendered, and while they had neither ammunition, artillery, troops
nor provisions to withstand a siege, they drew up their own
articles of capitulation,‡which were accepted, and on the 13th
November, 1775, at 9 o'clock, the Continental troops took
possession by the Recollet Gate,§ only, however, to retain
their position for a few brief months, when the old flag again

* This Medal is the only one thus far met with, bearing the word Mohigrans (Mohicans ?) on
the reverse. A similar medal with the word "Onondagas," has, however, been found. The
Medal here represented is now in the valuable collection owned by H. Mott, Esq., President
of the Numismatic and Antiquarian Society of Montreal.

† Brigadier General Richard Montgomery, was born in Ireland in 1737. He entered the
British Army, and served under Wolfe at Quebec; but subsequently entered the Continental
(American) Army, and was placed in command of the force sent to conquer Canada. On the
13th November, 1775, Montreal was captured; but he lost his life in the attack upon Quebec,
in December of the same year. See Autograph, Plate 8, fig. 4.

‡ See Appendix B.   § See Plate 6.

PLATE 10.

RECOLLETS   PARISH CHURCH   JESUITS   CITADEL HILL

RIVER ST LAWRENCE

MONTREAL IN 1760.

FROM AN OLD PRINT.

floated from " Citadel Hill." From this time onward, Montreal prospered, and extended its borders in every direction,
so much so, that in 1797, the city having o'erleaped its for-
mer bounds, and the walls having become a decided nui-
sance, it was resolved to remove them. The Lower Canada
House of Assembly, in 1801, consequently passed an Act

appointing the Hon. James McGill,* Hon. John Richardson,†

* Hon. James McGill was born in Glasgow, Scotland, on the 6th October, 1744. While a young
man he emigrated to Canada, and settled in Montreal, engaging successfully in commercial
pursuits. His integrity, public spirit, and practical good sense, gained for him the confidence
of his fellow citizens, and he was elected their representative in Parliament, and continued for
some years as such. He died at Montreal, on the 19th December, 1813, at the age of 69 years.
Not having any children, he bequeathed his beautiful estate of Burnside, with a sum of £10,000,
for the foundation of the University which now bears his name. See Portrait and Autograph,
above.

† Hon. John Richardson was for some years a member of the Executive and Legislative

and Jean Marie Mondelet, Esq., N.P.,‡ Commissioners, to remove them. The walls having been erected at the joint expense of the Government and Citizens, a similar partition
attended the cost of their removal, the expense being equally divided.

As we have previously stated, a considerable portion of the
land on which the walls were erected, had been taken without compensation. The Act passed in 1801, provided :
" That it is just and reasonable that the lands which the
said walls and fortifications now occupy, and which do not
belong to His Majesty, should be delivered up to the lawful
proprietors thereof, their heirs or assigns." The settlement
of claims under this Act required several years to complete,
and in the mean time, the Act was continued, until finally,
in 1817, the walls were entirely removed. A glance at the
map† will shew those acquainted with the present City,
that the walls extended along the river front from the
corner of the old barracks, to the foot of McGill Street, along
which it passed, enclosing part of the present Victoria
Square, thence along Fortification Lane, across the Champ
de Mars, onward through St. Louis Street, to Dalhousie
Square, and then returning to the barrack corner.

When the work of demolition was completed, the Commissioners proceeded to lay out a square, and wider street
on the western terminus of the city ; and, readily agreeing,
d cided to perpetuate the memory of their labours by con-

Councils of Lower Canada. He was distinguished during a residence of near fifty years in
th Province, by the rectitude and consistency of his conduct, by his spirit of enterprise in
promoting improvement, and by the most extensive benevolence. He was born at Portsoy, in
the County of Banff, North Britain, and emigrated to the Colonies (now the United States) in
1774, and came to Canada in 1787, where he attained great eminence as a merchant; and displayed, in his long career of public service, the talent with which he was endowed. He died
on the 18th of May, 1831, in the 77th year of his age. The Richardson Wing of the Montreal
General Hospital was erected to his memory, See Autograph, Plate 8, fig. 6.

* Jean Marie Mondelet, was son of Dominique Mondelet, a native of France, who came to
Canada under the French Government as Assistant Army Surgeon. Mr. J. M. Mondelet was
a prominent personage in politics, and represented Montreal East, in Parliament, during several
sessions. He was a Notary by Profession, and was much respected in the City. See Autograph, Plate 8, fig. 5.   † Plate 9.

PLATE 11.

VIEW OF MONTREAL IN 1803, SHEWING THE OLD WALLS ON THE RIVER FRONT, From a Scarce Print.

ferring their name on the square, (the present Victoria Square), which was accordingly named "Commissioners Square," and continued to be known as such until a few days before the Prince of Wales' arrival, when one of the Councillors very cleverly proposed to alter its name to Victoria Square, *in commemoration* of said visit. The Fortification Removal Commissioners readily came to an agreement respecting the name of their square, but seem to have had a little "tiff," over the name of the new street. Before they widened it, it was called St. Augustin Street. Mr McGill called it McGill Street, and entered it as such on the deed of homologation. Mr. Richardson contended, on the contrary, that it should be called after him, and did likewise on the deed. Mr. Mondelet also put in his claim, arguing with equal justice, that it should be known as Mondelet Street, and in his turn also entered it as such. It is hard to tell who decided the question between these three contestants, but the deed shows that Mr. Richardson's and Mr. Mondelet's names were erased, and Mr. McGill's allowed to remain.

While removing the old Fortifications, an interesting relic of early days was discovered in one of the bastions. The old French Halbard thus discovered, belongs to a period dating back to the very earliest history of the City, and we may picture to ourselves the French sentry bearing this weapon while pacing to and fro upon his beat within the old wooden palisades, or upon the ramparts of the more modern walls. This relic was formerly in the collection of Sir G. Duncan Gibb, M. D., Bart., (now of London), formerly an honored resident of Montreal. It was presented by him to the Natural History Society of Montreal.

By order of the Commissioners the old Citadel Hill was razed, and when, in 1821, the site was presented to the City by the Governor General, the Earl of Dalhousie,*the Square then opened, was in honor of the liberal donor, designated " Dalhousie Square," by which name it is still known.

It is difficult to say if any portion of the old French wall is still above ground. The water front of the Quebee Gate Barracks is supposed to be built upon a part of it, and is the only

OLD BARRACKS.

portion left, being with the old Barrack on Water Street, the only vestige remaining of French military power in this city. The Government store houses of the *ancien regime* were in the same part of the town, east of the Bonsecours Church ; and "owing to the venality of Varin, ' the Commissary of the Marine,' and Martel, ' the Storekeeper,' two gentlemen who displayed great talent in cheating the French Government out of its stores, and charging for them twice over, early received the name of *La Friponne*, a name which still adheres to the lane on which they abutted."

---

* George, ninth Earl of Dalhousie, was born in 1770, and succeeded to the title on the death of his father in November, 1787. He entered the army the same year as a Cornet in the 3rd Dragoon Guards, and during his military career rendered the most valuable service. In 1816, he was appointed Lieut.-General Commanding in Nova Scotia, and on the death of the Duke of Richmond, succeeded him as Governor of British North America, which high office he retained until 1828. He died at Dalhousie Castle, Scotland, on the 21st March, 1838. See Autograph, Plate 8, fig. 7.

At the present time, there stand on the line of Sherbrooke Street, (west of Guy Street,) two remarkable looking stone towers, having at the first glance, an appearance not unlike

OLD TOWERS AND COLLEGE.

the remains of old wind mills. These quaint looking circular towers, with their rough walls, contrast strangely with the more beautiful masonry of the massive walls of the immense structure in their rear, known as the Great Seminary. Yet we honor the "Gentlemen of the Seminary" for the feelings which have prompted them to retain these old landmarks. For over a century and a half, have these towers withstood the assaults of time, and in their early history they served to guard the entrance within the wall which surrounded the old "*Maison de Prêtres,*" as the first building was called. Within these towers have gathered, some of the early Priests, and their Indian converts, looking anxiously towards the dark forest by which they were surrounded, expecting, yet dreading the appearance of the treacherous and savage foe. Here also, the gentle Madame Bourgeoys* has sat, and taught the young Indian girls, and endeavored to

---

* Marguerite Bourgeoys, the pious and benevolent Founder of the Convent of the Congregation of Notre Dame at Montreal, was born at Troyes, in France, on the 15th April, 1620, and was brought to Canada in September, 1653, by Maisonneuve, who had been visiting France. She died full of days and honors on the 12th of January, 1700, aged 80 years. See Autograph, Plate 8, fig. 8.

impart to them some of that zeal which fired her own heart.*
How changed is the scene ! Now, villa and mansion sur-
round the spot, and there is nought of by gone days, save
these two solitary towers, the last remaining relics of the
" *Fort de la Montagne.*"

Though strictly speaking, the old fort does not come
within the compass of this work, still its connection with
the early settlement, is so intimate, that I feel justified in
thus dwelling upon its past history, and present appearance.

I shall now close by stating, that some years ago, plans
were prepared, by order of the British Government, for the
erection of most extensive and formidable batteries, and
other defences for the city. By those plans it was intended
that the works should extend from about two miles below
the city, on the opposite shore of the St. Lawrence, to the
foot of the Lachine Rapids, taking a curvelinear form, with
a radius of two miles from the river. These were to be
surrounded with a wet ditch, and have five bomb-proof forts,
each containing a small barracks and arsenal. A sixth fort
of superior size was to be erected on St. Helen's Island.
All these works were to be of stone, faced with earth. For
this object, land was acquired, but it is more than probable
that the stone pillars bearing the well known broad arrow
and the letters B. O., which serve to mark the boundary of
the purchased land, is all the stone work which will ever be
erected thereon by the Government. Let us hope that the
necessity may never arise for further expenditure, but that
learning to " bear and forbear," we may live at peace with
all, and cultivate only such feelings as shall forever remove
any apprehension of difficulty, or dispute between Canada and
its neighbors, or other nations.

---

* See Appendix C.

APPENDIX A.

CAPITULATION IN 1760.

The Articles of Capitulation were fifty-five in number, and in almost every instance were readily granted by Amherst. DeVaudreuil, however, endeavored to secure further concession, if possible, and urged the same through the officers charged with arranging the details. To his demand, the following letter was sent :

CAMP BEFORE MONTREAL,
7th Sept., 1760.

SIR,—Major Abercrombie has just communicated to me the letter which your Excellency has honored me with, in answer to that I have addressed you, with the conditions on which I expect the surrender of Canada. I have already had the honor to advise you that I shall not make any alteration. You will then be pleased to decide at once, and inform me in answer, whether you will accept them. Yes or no.

Sir, your Excellency's
Most humble and most obed. servant,

JEFF. AMHERST.

To the Terms of Capitulation, the Chevalier de Levis entered his protest, and asked Vaudreuil's permission to retire to St. Helen's Island with his troops, and there defend himself. When refused, he requested that such refusal should be forwarded in writing, and accordingly DeVaudreuil sent the following order :

"Whereas, the interests of the Colony does not permit

me to re_ect the conditions proposed by the English General, which are favorable to a country whose lot is confided to
me, I order Chevalier de Levis to conform himself to the
said capitulation, and to make the troops lay down their
arms."

VAUDREUIL.

Montreal, 8th Sept., 1760.

APPENDIX B.

CAPITULATION OF MONTREAL IN 1775.

. . . The inhabitants assembled, and the following articles
of capitulation were drawn up and presented to Montgomery, by a deputation of the most respectable citizens :

" 1st. That the citizens and inhabitants of Montreal, as
well individuals as religious orders and communities, without any exception, shall be maintained in the free possession
and enjoyment of their rights, goods and effects, movable
and immovable, of what nature soever they may be.

" 2nd. That the inhabitants, French and English, shall be
maintained in the free exercise of their religion.

"' 3rd. That trade in general, as well within the province
as in the upper countries, and parts beyond the seas, shall
be carried on freely as heretofore, and passports shall be
granted for that purpose.

" 4th. That passports shall be granted to those who may
want them for the different parts of this Province, or else-
where, on their lawful affairs.

" 5th. That the citizens and inhabitants of the town and
suburbs of Montreal, shall not be compelled, on any pre-
tence whatsoever, to take up arms against the Mother Country, nor to contribute in any manner towards carrying on,
war against her.

" 6th. That the citizens and inhabitants of the town and suburbs, or any other part of the country, who have taken up arms for the defence of this Province, and are taken prisoners, shall be set at liberty.

" 7th. That Courts of Justice shall be established for the determination of property ; and that the judge of the said Courts shall be elected by the people.

" 8th. That the inhabitants of the town shall not be subjected to lodge troops.

" 9th. That no inhabitant of the country, or savages, shall be permitted to enter the town until the Commandant shall have taken possession and provided for the security thereof.

(Signed,)

JOHN PORTEOUS.	PIERRE PANET.
RICHARD HUNTLEY.	PIERRE MEZIERE.
JOHN BLAKE.	ST. GEORGE DUPRE.
EDW. WM. GRAY.	LOUIS CARIGNANT.
JAMES FINLAY.	FRANCOIS MALHOIT.
JAMES McGILL.	PIERRE GUY. "

To this Montgomery returned the following written answer :

" I do hereby certify that the above articles were presented to me, to which I have given the following answers :

" The City of Montreal having neither ammunition, artillery, troops nor provisions ; and having it not in their power to fulfil one article of the treaty, can claim no title to a capitulation.

" The continental arms have a generous disdain of every act of oppression and violence ; they are come for the express purpose of giving liberty and security. The General therefore, engages his honor to maintain in the peaceable enjoyment of their property of every kind, the individual and religious communities of the city of Montreal.

" The inhabitants, whether English, French, or others, shall be maintained in the free exercise of their religion.

" The present unhappy contention between Great Britain and her colonies, puts it out of his power to engage for a freedom of trade to the Mother Country ; nor can he make a general promise of passports. As far as it consists with the safety of the troops and the public good, he shall be happy to promote commerce ; and for that purpose promises to grant passports to the Upper Countries when required.

" The General hopes to see such a virtuous provincial convention assembled, as will enter with zeal into every measure that can contribute to set the civil and religious rights of this and her sister colonies on a permanent foundation. He promises for himself that he will not compel the inhabitants of the town to take up arms against the Mother Country, or contribute towards the expenses of carrying on the present war.

The continental army came into this Province for its protection ; they therefore cannot consider its opposers as taking up arms for its defence.

" It is not in the General's power to engage for the return of prisoners. Motives of humanity will induce him to use his interest for their return to their families, provided it can be done without endangering the public safety. Speedy measures shall be taken for establishing Courts of Justice upon the most liberal plan, conformable to the British Constitution.

" The inhabitants shall not be burdened with troops, but when necessity requires it ; of which necessity, the General must be the judge.

" The inhabitants' of the country, and savages, shall not enter the town till the guards are posted.

" To-morrow morning, at nine o'clock, the continental troops shall take possession of the Recollet Gate. The proper officers must attend with the keys of all public stores, upon the Quarter-Master General, at nine o'clock, at the Recollet Gate.

"This engagement is understood and declared to be binding on any future commanding officer of the continental troops that may succeed me in this district.

(Signed,)   RICHARD MONTGOMERY,
Brigadier-General, Continental Army.

Montreal, 12th November, 1775."

————•————

APPENDIX C.

THE OLD TOWERS OF THE "FORT DE MESSIEURS."

Our gifted Canadian Poetess, Mrs. J. M. Leprohon, has made these towers the subject for a beautiful poem, from which we now quote, and we heartily respond to the sentiment expressed in the closing lines.

" On the eastern slope of Mount Royal's side,
In view of St. Lawrence' silvery tide,
Are two stone towers of masonry rude
With massive doors of time-darkened wood ;
Traces of loop-holes still show in the walls
Whilst softly across them the sun light falls ;
Around, stretch broad meadows, quiet and green
Where cattle graze—a fair, tranquil scene.

Those old towers tell of a time long past
When the red man roamed o'er these regions vast,
And the settlers—men of bold heart and brow,
Had to use the sword as well as the plough ;

When women, no lovelier now than then,
Had to do the deeds of undaunted men,
And had higher aims for each true warm heart
Than study of fashion's or toilet's art.

*   *   *   *

It was in those towers—the southern one—
Sister Margaret Bourgeoys, that sainted nun
Sat patiently teaching, day after day,
How to find Jesus—the blessed way,
Mid the daughters swarth of the forest dell,
Who first from her of a God heard tell ;
And learned the virtues that woman should **grace**
Whatever, might be her rank, or her race.

Here, too, in the chapel tower buried deep,
An Indian *brave* and his grand-child sleep,
True model of womanly virtues—she—
Acquired at Margaret Bourgeoys' knee ;
He, won unto Christ from his own dark creed,
From the trammels fierce of his childhood freed,
Lowly humbled his savage Huron pride
And amid the pale faces lived and died.

With each added year grows our city fair ;
Churches rich, lofty, and spacious square,
Villas and mansions of stately pride,
Embellish it now on every side ;
Buildings—old landmarks—vanish each day,
For stately successors to quick make way ;
But we pray from change, time may long leave free
The ancient towers of Ville Marie !

APPENDIX D,

KEY TO CHAMPLAIN'S MAP OF ISLAND OF MONTREAL, (PLATE 1.)

A—Small place which I got cleared. (Pointe a Callière.)

B—Small Pond. (Viger Square.)

C—Island where I caused a stone wall to be built. (Island Wharf.)

D—Brook where the boats are kept. (Now covered by Commissioners Street.)

E—Prairies where the Indians remain when they come into the country. (Point St. Charles.)

F—Mountains. (Belœil.)

G—Pond.

H—Mount Royal.

I —Small Brook. (Now called River St. Pierre.)

L—The Sault or Rapids.

M—Place where the Indians pass their canoes over land, going Northwards.

N—Place where one of our men, and an Indian were drowned.

O, P, Q, S, T, V, X—Islands.

Y—Prairies. (La Prairie.)

Z—Small River. (La Tortue River.)

2—Large and fine Island. (Nun's Island.)

3—Shallow places where the water is much agitated.

4—Prairies, at times covered with water.

5—Shoals.

6—Small Island.

7—Rocks.

8—St. Helen's Island.

9—Small barren Island.

www.ingramcontent.com/pod-product-compliance
Lightning Source LLC
Chambersburg PA
CBHW031752090426
42739CB00008B/982